The World's
Toughest
Golf
Holes

Featuring many American Golfing Nightmares

Tom Hepburn & Selwyn Jacobson

SAINT

American Edition: 1997

Concept: Tom Hepburn and Selwyn Jacobson
Text: Tom Hepburn
Illustrations: John Cole, Tom Folwell, Grant Hanna, Rod Proud
Printed in Hong Kong through Colorcraft Ltd
Distributed in the United States by
Seven Hills Book Distributors, Cincinatti, Ohio.

© 1995 Saint Publishing Ltd
ISBN 0-908697-65-1

SAINT PUBLISHING LTD
P.O.Box 8157, Symonds Street
56 Mt Eden Road
Auckland, 1003, New Zealand

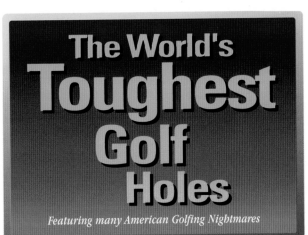

The World's
Toughest
Golf
Holes

Featuring many American Golfing Nightmares

CONTENTS

INTRODUCTION

What better way to introduce this extraordinary collection of hiatus hernia inducers for the highly handicapped than to offer a quote from that Sage of Golfing Sages, James Braid McBaffie himself, who wrote in his now famous 'Little Tartan Book' . . .

"All the world's a golf course,

and on it Men play 18 holes".

Ah, the sheer poetry!

The balance of the 1347 stanzas of that epic epigram are, of course, history, which is probably the best place for them. But the genius lives on in the concept, design, and unadulterated playing pleasures of a level of golf course architecture which has become internationally accepted as 'The McBaffie Style'.

What little lad at his father's knee, practicing his short game with a bit of coal on the hearthrug, cut-down cleek clutched (using the Vardon grip of course) in chubby fingers, hasn't heard a wistful parental voice contemplate 'what might have been, if only . . .'

But enough!

The reality lies in the pages before you. Turn now and peruse this latest sampling from the Great Holes Of (McBaffie style) Golf.

And never, ever again regret a double bogey at your local track.

Washington U.S.A

Grand Canyon Country Club 10th hole

580 yards par 5

Rum Rim

As drop shots go, this is one of the hardest to judge. Perspective tends to affect one's judgement and rarely does a player choose enough club to clear the canyon rim, much less reach the fairway, far down to the left.

From both tees the view is stupendous, and it is this, as much as dithering over club choice, which often builds up a backlog.

There is no real problem, though, for once they get away off the tee, players tend to disappear quietly into the depths of the canyon, often for several days at a time, before reappearing dishevelled and tired, and grateful to be back alive.

Arizona, USA

Muriwai Golf Club 9th hole

185 yards par 3

Gully

Muriwai has had a long and, sad to say, generally losing battle with erosion, a problem exemplified here on the 9th hole of the original course (seldom played now but worth a visit if for no other reason than the bracing ozone).

Where once a drive would roll sedately onto the green, now it is carry all the way. And as though to rub salt in the wound — 'salt' being the *mot juste* in this case — a colony of gannets has made a permanent home on the green.

This in itself would not have been too bad, had not Murdo Bewes, convenor of the Match Committee and an ardent ornithologist, become so enraged at continual and feeble jokes about birdies that he designated the entire colony an integral part of the course.

Which makes for interesting putting!

Auckland , New Zealand

Lake Mungo Golf Club 3rd hole

330 yards par 4

China Balls

To make golf balls which fly higher, lower, straighter, further, last longer and cost less, has long been man's natural cause in life, but it wasn't until the intrepid Scottish (what else?) explorer Mungo Park experimented in detail with the then unproven Chinese ball that at least five out of the six aims were realised.

Alas, 'long-lasting' proved unattainable, since these 'great balls of China' would shatter either on club impact, or on a good day, on the first bounce.

Ah well, what are explorers for, if not to show us which paths have dead-ends?

New South Wales, Australia

Tingerpuk Golf Course 5th hole

330 yards par 4

Frozen Fish

Midnight golf is no longer a thing to wonder at, not now when public courses around the country have their floodlights at every hole, and players have to go around in groups of five, and those who stray from the fairways have to drop back on again (no penalty) just to keep the game moving fast enough to give everyone who wants to play some small chance.

But, north of the Arctic Circle, there is no such rush since Midnight Golf was invented (by sous-chef Chukchi McBaffie, who was marooned by Amundsen for practicing driving off the poop deck instead of pickling herrings for dinner). The game flourishes on courses where there are never queues at the first tee.

And where a pickled herring may be had for the asking, back at the clubhouse.

Alaska, U.S.A

Waka-Tips Golf Club 1st hole

1850 yards par 4

Re Mark-a-Ball

Not as long a '4' as you'd think from the card, as the drive tends to eat up the distance even when fluffed, and the approach is almost always within mid-iron range. But a nail-biting start to a nerve-wracking round nevertheless.

First timers here are asked to use the 14" spikes (from the pro shop at ¥85000 the set) as the teeing ground snow is often quite icy. And deep!

The name of this hole derives from the very sensible local practice which allows the golfer to mark the ball position, usually with a spade, or an ice-pick, before striking it. If the ball is topped (usually down into several feet of snow) another may be placed in the recently-sculpted crater with no penalty.

One of the many benefits of mountain golf!

Queenstown, New Zealand

Urquhart Castle Municipal Links 1st hole

85 yards par 3

Nessie Dormie?

The current British penchant for turning otherwise useless old ruins into expensive Country Clubs has yet to hit Scotland, but up there they are doing their best to cope with the immense waiting lists around the country.

The clubhouse here at Urquhart Castle, on Loch Ness, is typical of the kind of money being lavished on such facilities. Despite its attractive setting, and being 3,952nd in line for the British Open, membership is small. Perhaps because of the added lateral hazard at this tricky little opening hole?

It was here that a representative of the R & A, called in to provide a Definition (later to be listed under "Governing Authority; Serpents — sea; consumption by") ventured too close to the shoreline while pacing out a dropping zone, disappeared into a slight morning mist, and was never seen again.

Scotland, United Kingdom

Bungle Bungle Golf Club 8th hole

610 yards par 5

Criss-Cross

No prizes for guessing why this golf club got its name, but the 'how' is interesting.

A mix-up on the design front saw two golf architects hired instead of one, each with his own idea on which side of the gorge the course should run. By the time the Committee realised the two men wouldn't talk to each other, and had gone their separate ways, nine holes had been laid out along each rim.

The resulting criss-crossing, though entertaining to begin with, becomes a bit wearisome on the legs, as there are no funds available for bridges. A donation box remains strangely empty, back at the clubhouse.

Perhaps because very few visitors ever get that far?

Western Australia, Australia

Neuschwannstein Country Club 18th hole

185 yards par 3

Swan Song

It is a constant source of relief to the German people, so often criticised for their meek acceptance of authority, inability to cope with lateral thinking and general stodginess, to be able to point, with justifiable pride, at Ludwig Wittelsbach, creator of the least ordinary golf course in the world.

Ludwig, who also doubled as King, became fed up with wars (he never could work out whether to support Austria or Prussia) and got together with brother Otto — who was ever a sandwich short of a picnic — and his mate Dick Wagner, a popular song writer. Between them they designed the fascinating 18-hole course at/in/over and through Ludwig's holiday home.

It hasn't yet featured the German Open, but it certainly pulls in the tourists!

Bavaria, Germany

Red Rock Canyon Country Club 7th hole

480 yards par 4

Hole in Hole

It was typical of that cantankerous old Scottish pro, Reekie McSwete, to revenge himself so savagely on the generous members of the R.R.C. Disabled Veterans Committee, but perhaps, looking back, he had a point. After all, he gave a lifetime of selfless devotion to the club: its greens and fairways would have been like a barren desert if not for McSwete's brother, the egregious Pukie; the clubhouse extension money would never have been so unpredictably squandered; and the much publicised *intacta* status of the ladies' Captain Virginia Bywater, would not . . . no, no, such comment here is unseemly!

Yet revenge was the word, for with his last, dying command, old Reekie drew up the design for the new 7th green and brother Pukie saw that it was a *fait accompli.*

The odd circuit pro passes this way, but even so the record for this hole remains at 183. Well, what can you expect of an odd pro?

Utah, U.S.A

24

Swanage Municipal Links 14th hole

275 yards par 3

Old Harry's Rocks

The love affair of Harry Penhaligon and Deirdre McBaffie – a torrid business which had lace curtains twitching from Bognor Regis to the Bill, came to its inevitable end on Swanage Links, during the Mixed Pairs Chalice.

Deirdre, paired with a certain Mr. T. Morris, fell for him during the first nine. Harry, a Dorset man to his last, long vowel, could not compete with Tom's erotic brogue, and had to watch, silently seething, as Morris nonchalently went par, eagle, birdie, par until Deidre was all but writhing at his feet.

At last, berserk with frustrated lust and rage (not a good combination for a steady take away), Harry took to Morris with his driver. Alas, he failed to spot a loose impediment, tripped over the edge of the green, and plummeted into the broiling foam. Young Morris, almost (but not quite) looking up from a long putt, murmured, "Puir auld Harry – aff his rocks", before sinking yet another birdie.

Dorset, United Kingdom

Cooloola Municipal Links 17th hole

485 yards par 5

Hats Off

That familiar golfing term 'A Real Cool Lulu' (well, familiar enough between Cootharaba and Tin Can Bay anyway) became such an 'in' phrase the local National Park was named after it – thanks in a funny way to Harry Spring and wee Tommy 'Gympie' Hiley, who fought such a bitter grudge match here that the course was almost closed.

Although it seems comical in retrospect to reflect that a five foot six one-legged 33-handicapper could actually out-play a hulking Victorian Rules Plus 1 stalwart in the Captain's Cup final, those present at that gory debacle at the 17th (they were all square, both in the big fairway bunker with their 15ths, side by side, equal distance from the pin and decided to hit simultaneously) agreed unanimously that if it hadn't been for Gympie's one good leg sinking into soft sand, Harry's follow-through would have decapitated him. As it was, it sliced his brand new $75.00 Great White Shark hat in half and Gympie stormed off the course in protest - and of course lost the match.

Queensland, Australia

28

Waimangu Golf Club 11th hole

500 yards par 5

Steam Hit

This delightful course, set in a thermal valley to the south of Rotorua, has alas finally taken down its ' visitors welcome' sign, and is now available only to golfing parties accompanied by a registered guide.

The cause of this mixed blessing was the annual visit of the Whakarewarewa ladies team, led by the indomitable if sturdy Bessie Peasmarch (then a mere 325lbs).

Bessie, on her way across the tepid mineral pool to the 11th green — the waters of which had so often in the past proved beneficial to her bunions — accidentally dropped her wedge down a fissure.

The resultant haemorrhage to the earth's crust caused the depth of the pool to rise four feet and the temperature to 200 degrees fahrenheit, the creation of a great new golf hole, and the sudden need for guides.

Rotorua, New Zealand

Haleakala Golf & Country Club 12th hole

440 yards par 4

Never the Twain

This idyllic scene scarcely suggests that only 120 years ago this course, then in its infancy, was a diamond in the rough, lacking the multiple sports facilities available today. Those who know their golfing history will recall the words of Mark Twain (never a good golfer — but as a stroke player he made a good writer). His enthusiasm, however, was not in doubt, as the following quotation from the unexpurgated version of *Roughing It* shows.

Twain's favorite spot in all of Hawaii was up here at the 10,000' level, Maui's highest point.

"... *yawning dead crater, into which we would practice our short approach shots from our perch and see them go careening down the almost perpendicular sides, bounding three hundred feet at a jump; kicking up dust clouds wherever they struck; diminishing to our view as they sped farther into the distance; growing invisible, finally, and only betraying the course by faint little puffs of dust; and coming to a halt at last in the bottom of the abyss* (now the long 14th: Ed) *two thousand five hundred feet down from where they started.*

It was magnificent sport. We wore ourselves out at it!"

Maui, Hawaii, U.S.A

Black Canyon Golf Club
4th, 5th & 6th holes

187 yards
par 3s

Triple T's

Locals are proud to point out to visitors this astonishing, if little-known club. It is probably the only one in the world to boast not only a triple tee position, but one which services three identically-distanced holes. (The tall column in the foreground is, in fact, the seventh tee – the green out of sight to the left).

Because this is a potential bottleneck on busy days, a local rule allows players to add two shots to any drive which actually bounces onto a green, regardless of where the ball finishes.

This keeps the field moving briskly, an advantage in these days of slow play. And it helps to keep scores, which may otherwise attain a disreputable proportion, down to an acceptable level!

Colorado, U.S.A

Flodigarry Links
5th hole

470 yards
par 4

Dire Strait

Skye's — and probably Scotland's — narrowest course runs tantalizingly along these beautiful cliffs.

Reasonably flat (if you can hit straight), easy to par (if you can hit straight), no hazards or trees to speak of (if you can hit straight).

But — the fence line on the left indicates Out of Bounds, the steepish slope to the right means loss of distance if you slice, and the sloping tees, a feature of this course, all contribute to making it just that little bit tougher. To hit straight.

Not too tough, however, for young Garry Kyle — or 'Bloody Garry' as he was affectionately nicknamed after the incident on the 5th which saw him take 17 to get back up on the fairway — and that was climbing attempts, not shots — after his initial fall to the rocks below.

They breed golfers tough up there!

Scotland, United Kingdom

Maryvale Golf Club 9th hole

492 yards par 4

Chamber Pot

Out in the Territory, men often have great difficulty completing 18 holes without diving from time to time to seek relief behind the nearest monolith, such is the number of chilled tubes required to stave off dehydration.

But how to avoid embarrassing the ladies during mixed foursomes?

Old Randy Finke, a pillar of local society, found the answer. Now, during such events, each man must carry an official club chamberpot.

For visitors and forgetful members, spares are kept here at the 9th — hence the name.

Northern Territory, Australia

Mt. Taranaki Golf Club
8th hole

430 yards
par 4

The Fantham Striker

When Bob Ridge challenged Fennimore 'Far-Out' Fantham to a long drive competition, spectators (and there were many who knew of the prowess of these two scratch golfers) were aghast to learn that the men were to hit from the edge of the 8th green — in fact off Shark's Tooth itself!

Nevertheless a fair crowd wended its way up to the spot to cheer the lads. But imagine their surprise when Bob decided to hit down the sunlit ridge (left) and 'Far-Out' over and onto the small peak (right)!

The result? Well, Bob's ball rolled further, but Fantham, clearly at his peak, hit the 7th green on the full, and was declared winner.

Taranaki, New Zealand

Loch Ard Municipal Links
7th hole

210 yards
par 3

'Ard Cheese

In the late 19th century, a stroke of luck brought this now popular course into being. Given the prevailing stormy ocean which pulverizes the Port Campbell coastline, it was only a matter of time before one of the hundreds of shipwrecked mariners (this was a favorite dropping-off point) turned out to be a keen golfer.

And so, in the fullness of time, Lord Ard of Eirein found himself stranded on these lovely shores.

Immediately after he had established the obligatory Caledonian Society, and distillery, he set himself to designing this attractive links.

Victoria, Australia

Yellowstone Golf Club 16th hole

450 yards par 4

White Wash

When the idea was first mooted for a championship standard golf course to be laid out across the Yellowstone River (12 times over 18 holes as it turned out) the US Bureau of Golf Course Reclamation came under much criticism.

But, like government departments everywhere, it simply ignored public sentiment and went ahead regardless, doubling both staff and budget every six months in accordance with Parkinson's Law 14c.

(A government department expands in direct proportion to the number of people available to be employed by it).

Today, as we all know, this is one of the key courses on the High West (above 5,000 feet) Circuit.

Wyoming, U.S.A

Lamington Falls Country Club 11th hole

110 yards par 3

Dropsy

With over 500 cataracts to choose from, it is little wonder that water features in several instances on this, the only Queensland course made up of 18 consecutive drop shot holes.

If it seems to the casual observer that the teeing area here on the 11th is set a trifle close to the brink (some vertigo-prone visitors have been known to lie on their stomachs and cue the ball over) it must be remembered that, for such a stroke as this, weight distribution should favor the back foot.

Interestingly, many players seem to prefer the clubhouse as an alternative, since it is but a 5-minute stroll from the 11th tee (though an awkward 50 minute stretcher ride from the green below).

Queensland, Australia

Loch Laich Golf Club 1st hole

150 yards par 3

Castled

As the sun sinks slowly into the misty Highland west, and a plaintive pibroch skips and bounces over the limpid loch like a long, low 1-iron, the gentle splash of oar in water tells the passer-by that old 'Stalker' Strachan is out practicing again.

The Laird, owner and (only) member of this, the world's smallest Golf Club, takes the game seriously. From the first (and only) tee he takes his 7 (and only) iron and hits his (yes you've guessed it), only ball across to the first (and only) green.

He then rows over, winding in the string as he goes, putts out, rows back, tees up and starts all over again.

Dedication! Perseverance!

The very essence of golf!!

Scotland, United Kingdom

Fitzroy Falls Country Club 3rd hole

195 yards par 3

Wire-Less

Putting out on the 2nd is no mean feat here, but the real test of a golfer's will is the tee shot on the 3rd, where a proper follow-through to draw a 3-wood (at least) is essential if the long carry is to be achieved.

Fitzroy Baye-Morton, younger son of the Club's founder, old 'Bugsy' Baye-Morton, suffered not only from advanced in-growing toenails, but acute acrophobia. But he was keen, and prided himself he'd never failed to complete a full round.

His only recourse here was to tie himself to each tee peg with No. 8 wire, a somewhat restricting device for the full shoulder turn, but as good a way as any of remaining alive after striking the ball.

Until the day the wire snapped!

Intrepid to the end, Fitz plunged the spiked tee pegs through the toes of his shoes, and, thinking himself thus firmly rooted (how true!) made a valiant swing.

New pegs were of course supplied by the next day.

New South Wales, Australia

50

Little Home Country Club 9th hole

440 yards par 4

Ben's Doom

Laid out on the traditional 'nine out, nine in' basis the 9th here is about as far out – and as far up – as you can get. In fact, just a bit too far up for the club's siren, sexy Selina St Clair, whose trendy tartan mini-golfing skirt was the direct cause of the 187 taken by her playing partner of the day, wee Benny Lomond, who, as any gentleman would, assisted the young lass up to the ladies' tee.

The 73-year-old Benny unaccountably started to shake at the knees, then in several other places, and try as he might he just could not make proper contact with his ball. He didn't do too badly, shooting his age to reach the shore, until a topped wedge into the lake brought final disaster.

But the really bad news? Selina, a modest lass at heart, took to wearing pants.

Tasmania, Australia

Tarawera Country Club Inc.
9th hole

550m
par 5

Oh, Blow!

When this hole was introduced to what was then a fairly mundane layout, back in 1886, it caused something of an explosion in the local golfing world, but soon it became an accepted part of the course, and an adventure to be looked forward to as the culmination of the outward nine.

Originally the green was up on the northern lip, but as the average time taken by a foursome to complete the hole worked out at just over five hours, the course committee decided to re-site the green down in the valley. This was a good move, and now any shot struck sufficiently hard will bounce its way down and, with a bit of luck, end up on the putting surface.

The downside, of course, is the inevitable long walk back up to the par 5 10th tee (distant right, green distant left) but from there on the going is even. Or as even as possible, given the course is on top of an active volcano. . .

Rotorua, New Zealand

Hamersley Country Club 11th hole

160 yards par 3

Fortesque's Folly

Some 2000 million years ago, when the earth's crust first settled and solidified, the basis was laid here for future golf course architecture.

And no, there weren't any golf courses then, silly. They first appeared much later during the warm Devonian, or English Links, period.

This fine example of a natural hole needs the perfect drive if par is to be possible — no amount of scrabbling will rescue anything less. Not too high, not too low, not too hard lest the ball rebound off the back of the green and down into the casual water. From where, even with a free drop, bogey or worse looms.

CROC TRAP

Western Australia, Australia

Nome Country Club 3rd hole

1086 yards par 3

Doglegs

Do not, gentle reader, be put off by this seemingly longish par 3. Up here in Alaska golf balls tend to travel further, especially along the ground, and even more especially when they are correctly struck along a Tarod trench.

This aid to better golfing (Alaska style at least) is a narrow track about a foot wide where the snow is compressed – usually by a team of assistant greenkeepers wielding specially flattened putters – and which extends from tee to green *although not always in a straight line.*

Idi Tarod, the Ugandan/Russian who invented this system, also pioneered the use of a sled and husky team as a replacement for electric buggies.

Seems they tend to start better in temperatures under sixty below.

Alaska, U.S.A

Bellfield Country Club 17th hole

350 yards par 3

Grumpy's Revenge

Mention the 17th within the hearing of old Grumpy 'Gramps' Guthrie, club secretary for 37 years and holder of the record for driver hurling, and you can be guaranteed a swift riposte.

Ever since that long-ago day when Gramps stood up on the newly formed tee to hit the inaugural ball, and fell off backwards after his 14th air shot, he has sought revenge.

First, through sheer influence, he had the fairway planted over. Then he had 'mounds' built around the green. Then he had the hole lengthened to allow only for his own prodigious distance off the tee. And then, when even he grew too old to hit the green, he had the tee marker surreptitiously altered, to confuse visitors.

He is even suspected of altering the par sign!

Australia

Faulty Tower Golf Club 10th hole

220 yards par 4

Pisa Puer

The famous Sicilian professional and part-time tenor Arno Palermo not only designed this lovely course, but introduced it into what was then a revolution in teaching techniques.

This elevated practice tee was built a short wedge high and a medium putt out of the perpendicular on Arno's specific instructions. He emphasised the psychological benefit to beginners of 'getting the ball in the air quickly' and thought this the best way to do it. Indeed this scheme worked very well, until the sad day when young Luciano 'Unlucky' Pisano leaned too far into a ball and swung himself over the edge after it.

Arno was intrigued to note that both ball and 'Unlucky' fell to the ground at similar speeds, but before he could experiment further, the tee was banned to beginners, eventually becoming integrated into the course proper.

Pisa, Italy

Nambung Golf Club
7th hole

404 yards
par 4

The Painted Veil

The more literary readers will of course, recognise the name of this astonishing little par 4 as deriving from the day Somerset (Wee Willie) Maugham played here as part of a promotion tour for a forthcoming, but yet un-named collection of short stories. His playing partner was Rodriguez Nambung-Smythe, club captain and local cretin.

On being told the area was known as 'The Painted Desert', Willie — who had just putted out for a new hole record of 83 and was feeling so damned good about it he had started kissing his caddy (again) — waxed suddenly poetic, and cried aloud "This painted vale, for which those who love golf, live!"

Roddy, typically, misheard, yet his hastily scribbled note served later not only to give the famous author's new work — but also the hole itself — a name!

Western Australia, Australia

Cascades Country Club 7th hole

350 yards par 4

No Rain 'Ere

There's Mt. Ranier, the suburb of Washington D.C., there's Mt. Ranier the snow-capped peak in Washington state, and there's Hiram Q. Ranier III, golfer extraordinaire, professional-elect to Monaco (though no one's told the Prince yet).

Hiram, last but by no means least, is the man who not only discovered the series of ice caves which make up this unusual course, but is the one instrumental in convincing the greens committee to provide a courtesy oilskin to all visitors. One to each four suffices, since attending the flagstick (a tricky task at best) becomes nigh on unacceptable when icy water is dripping down one's neck.

And a final word of advice here — beware the lofted approach to the green, as ricochets can prove harmful to your health — and score!

Washington, U.S.A

66

Nugget Point
Golf Club
18th hole

625 yards
par 5

Slope
of Despair

Though the seams of gold which ran (still run?) through various bits of New Zealand no longer pull the punters in, one of the spin-offs from the 'Rush of 89' still does! When rumour had it the off-shore rocks here were solid gold, you couldn't see Stewart Island for flying dirt and flashing picks and shovels. People poured in by the two's and three's, mainly unemployed greasy lookers from the Mosgiel mills.

The 'Golden Nuggets', as they were first called, may have failed to make many millionaires, but the resultant diggings made one – scratch handicapper Cluny Kaimataitai, then beach warden at Cannibal Bay, who quickly saw the golf course potential.

Nugget Point, with its trendy clubhouse, is now one of the most popular country courses south of Pollocks Hill.

Southland, New Zealand

Yosemite Valley Golf Club
9th hole

550 yards
par 5

The Three Brothers

In golf, as in life, good things often come in threes. Alas, not so this ill-fated hole, now widely known as Three Brothers Rock.

Samuel, Arnold and Walter Tuolumne, all members of the Social Committee (they ought to have known better!) foolishly accepted an alcohol-induced bet one evening to play the first nine in moonlight. All went well for eight holes, then tragedy struck in the access tunnel.

Arnie, leading the way as usual, slipped just as he was short of the green and slid backwards. He collected Sam and Walter and, together and gaining momentum, they flew out of the tunnel entrance at a speed at which even Cresta Run devotees would flinch.

They were never seen again, and a small plaque, discreetly placed at the tunnel entrance, cautions visitors not to drink and drive.

Except on the practice tee.

California, U.S.A

Kalbarri Municipal Links
3rd hole

566 yards
par 5

Ring of Confidence

Reminiscent in so many respects of the famous 18th at Pebble Beach, this intriguing hole adds a dimension — unknown to California's finest — to that most perplexing of all golf shots, the chip and run. Given your 2nd stays out of the sea, and your lie allows for at least part contact, beware the lofted approach!

Designed by the not terribly talented Edinburgh immigrant Murchison McBaffie for a land where a euro doesn't have a thick accent and grow grapes, this hole and its approach need careful thought.

Too high, and you're in trouble; through the green, and you're in trouble; play short and . . . well, you get the idea.

Western Australia, Australia

Hell's Mouth Country Club 13th hole

285 yards par 3

Swingers

From Godrevy to Portreath there is no sight more stimulating to a golfer than the view across the seaward holes of this lovely South England course.

However, on a breezy October day (though winds seldom exceed 180mph) the normally enjoyable stroll across to some of the greens becomes a trifle hazardous; the bridges tend to swing more than the players and quite a few trundlers, not to mention caddies, are tossed into the foaming brine like leaves from a tree. And when a gust comes from off-shore, some even leave from the tees.

This is the kind of hole where a competent caddy can earn his tip, given that he's taken the trouble to gain his life-saving badge during training (part of the official requirements since 1903, the year membership dropped to 18 during a single stormy afternoon).

Southern England, United Kingdom

Hidden City Country Club 16th hole

85 yards par 3

Twin Peaks

In the Australian Outback, golfers take their game seriously, and are unaccustomed to the excesses of course refinements so prevalent in the cities. Such aids as pitons, crampons, and rope ladders are seldom used, and irrelevancies such as pathways, caddy carts, graded rough and (horrors!) fairway sprinklers are scorned; if you can't climb up to the greens with a full set on your back, you shouldn't play, is the attitude.

Imagine then the derision poured upon the Twin Peaks course committee when they insisted on introducing a swing bridge "For the convenience of visitors and the chronologically disadvantaged"!

One good thing to come out of this was the reduction of the standard scratch to 98.6. But even now no self-respecting member under 50 would deign to use the bridge when a perfectly satisfactory rope is available.

Northern Territory, Australia

Percé Golf Club 11th hole

170 yards par 3

Percé's Point

In his 'Elegy Written in a Fairway Sandtrap' diminutive Thomas LeGris evokes one of golf's continuing magic moments when he writes . . .

"Now fades the glimmering landscape on the Greens

And in the clubhouse Golfers cold beers hold

Save where a Titleist wheels its droning flight

And muttered curses hint at duffs untold".

Thomas, on 36 has never owned a full set of clubs; nor ever made par in his life. Yet if you were to suggest that his was perhaps an 'ignoble strife', he'd fetch you one with his driving iron.

He can often be seen, perched on the tee watching other golfers here at the short 11th at sunset, clearly beguiled partly by the romance of the evening, partly by the flask of Canadian Club which never leaves his bag. At times he will call out merrily, after a particularly savage slice, *"Quatre!"* Or even *"A bas les Québecois!"* (his mother was Spanish) when a ball fails to reach the green and falls, lost forever, into the sea. Such simple pleasures gained at small expense: a lesson to us all.

Canada

SAINT

Distributed in the United States by Seven Hills Book Distributors.